A Note to Parents and Teachers

DK READERS is a compelling reading programme for children, designed in conjunction with leading literacy experts, including Cliff Moon M.Ed., Honorary Fellow of the University of Reading. Cliff Moon has spent many years as a teacher and teacher educator specializing in reading and has written more than 140 books for children and teachers. He reviews regularly for teachers' journals.

Beautiful illustrations and superb full-colour photographs combine with engaging, easy-to-read stories to offer a fresh approach to each subject in the series. Each DK READER is guaranteed to capture a child's interest while developing his or her reading skills, general knowledge, and love of reading.

The five levels of DK READERS are aimed at different reading abilities, enabling you to choose the books that are exactly right for your child:

Pre-level 1: Learning to read
Level 1: Beginning to read
Level 2: Beginning to read alone
Level 3: Reading alone
Level 4: Proficient readers

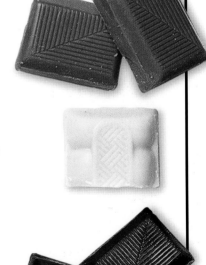

The "normal" age at which a child begins to read can be anywhere from three to eight years old, so these levels are only a general guideline.

No matter which level you select, you can be sure that you are helping your child learn to read, then read to learn!

LONDON, NEW YORK, MUNICH,
MELBOURNE, AND DELHI

Series Editor Deborah Lock
Art Editor Sadie Thomas
DTP Designer Almudena Díaz
Production Alison Lenane
Picture Researcher Sarah Pownall
Jacket Designer Nina Tara
Illustrator Peter Dennis
Indexer Lynn Bresler

Reading Consultant
Cliff Moon, M.Ed.

Published in Great Britain by Dorling Kindersley Limited
80 Strand, London WC2R 0RL
4 6 8 10 9 7 5
A Penguin Company

Copyright © 2005 Dorling Kindersley Limited

A CIP record for this book is
available from the British Library

ISBN-13: 978-1-4053-0387-3

Colour reproduction by Colourscan, Singapore
Printed and bound in China by L. Rex Printing Co. Ltd.

The publisher would like to thank the following for their kind
permission to reproduce their photographs.
a=above, b=below, c=centre, l=left, r=right, t=top.
Jacket Images Front: **Photolibrary.com:** Paul Poplis.
The Advertising Archive: 45br. akg-images: 23t. **Alamy Images:** Andre
Jenny 33b; G.P Bowater 36t. **The Art Archive:** Bodleian Library
Oxford/The Bodleian Library 15b; Dagli Orti 14b; Mireille Vautier 11c;
Musee Bouilhet-Christofle Paris/Dagli Orti 23b; Museo de America
Madrid/Dagli Orti 13br. **www.bridgeman.co.uk:** Museo de America,
Madrid 18; The Stapleton Collection 15tr. **Chip Clark:** 6-7b(midge), 7tl,
34br. **Corbis:** 38b; Bettmann 22, 26, 47t; Bob Krist 8t; Christine Osborne
25; Joe McDonald 33tr; Kevin Schafer 7r; Reuters 5c, 21. **DK Images:**
Copyright CONCULTA-INAH-MEX. Authorized reproduction by the
Instituto Nacional de Antropologia e Historia. 11b; Copyright Judith
Miller & Dorling Kindersley/Noel Barrett Antique & Auctions House
27br; Copyright Judith Miller & Dorling Kindersley/T W Conroy, NY. 43t.
Dolfin Chocolat: 44. **Mary Evans Picture Library:** 12, 29br. **Fairtrade
Foundation:** 36br. **Getty Images:** Angelo Cavalli 9; Juan Silva 43b.
Grenada Chocolate Company: 39b. **Hulton Archive/Getty Images:**
Haywood Magee/Picture Post 32b. **Kobal Collection:** Warner Bros 47br.
Lindt & Sprungli (International) AG: 29c, 42t. **Lonely Planet Images:**
Greg Elms 46b. **N.H.P.A.:** Haroldo Palo Jr 10tl. **Photolibrary.com:** Brian
Hagiwara 28br. **Plamil Foods Ltd:** 35br. **Eric Postpischil:**
http://edp.org/Germany/Koeln.html/ Imhoff-Stollwerck-Museum 27tr, 31c.
Rex Features: The Travel Library 4. **Karen Robinson:** 37. **Science Photo
Library:** Dr Morley Read 6l. **Earl Taylor:** Trade card from the private
collection of Earl Taylor, Dorchester, Massachusetts 24b. **Topfoto.co.uk:**
5br. **TransFair USA:** 36bc. **Zefa Visual Media:** G.Baden 45c; Miep van
Damm 28bl.

All other images © Dorling Kindersley Limited
For further information see: www.dkimages.com

Discover more at

www.dk.com

Contents

DK READERS

READING 3 ALONE

The Story of Chocolate

Written by C. J. Polin

A Dorling Kindersley Book

Chocolate trees

Do you like chocolate? Most people would answer "Yes!" We eat an average of 9 kilograms (20 lbs) of chocolate per person per year. That's about 180 chocolate bars each! But where does chocolate come from, and how is it made into the sweet, delicious treats that we love to eat?

The story of chocolate begins in the rainforest, where cacao (ka-KOW) trees grow. Pods grow on the cacao trees and inside the pods are seeds called cocoa (KO-ko) beans. These cocoa beans are the magic ingredient in chocolate.

Dried cocoa beans

Theobroma cacao

In 1753, the Swedish scientist Linnaeus gave the cacao tree its scientific name, *Theobroma cacao*, meaning "food of the gods". It was well known that he liked chocolate!

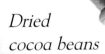

Cacao trees grow in the hot, damp shade under the leafy canopy of the tallest trees in the rainforest. There, the cacao trees blossom with pink and white flowers. These flowers grow straight from the trunk and main branches. Tiny insects called midges carry pollen between the blossoms, fertilising them so cocoa pods will grow.

A midge sitting on the tip of a pin.

Only a few of the hundreds of blossoms develop into cocoa pods. Like the blossoms, the pods grow straight from the trunk and branches of the tree. Many cacao trees grow both blossoms and pods all year round.

In about four months, the cocoa pods grow to the size of melons. It takes another month before they are fully ripe. The colour of the ripe pods ranges from yellow to dark red. The pods are hard and must be split open to show the beans. Each pod contains about 40 cocoa beans surrounded by sticky white pulp. These are the precious beans that make chocolate.

Who first discovered that these strange-looking beans, from these strange-looking trees, could be used to make such a delicious treat?

An ancient treat

Cacao trees grow in the ancient area called Mesoamerica, which includes southern Mexico and Central America. Many experts believe that the first people to crack open a cocoa pod and use the bean were the ancient Olmecs, who lived from about 1200 to 200 BCE.

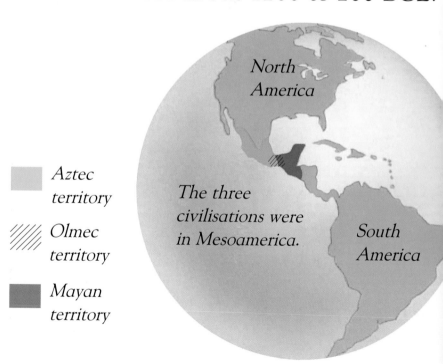

Aztec territory

Olmec territory

Mayan territory

North America

The three civilisations were in Mesoamerica.

South America

The Mayans were the first people to plant the beans of wild cacao trees. This was the beginning of cocoa farming. In return for other goods, the Mayans traded cocoa beans to the Aztecs, whose lands were too dry to grow cacao trees.

Olmec monuments

Much of Mesoamerican culture is said to originate from the ancient Olmecs. In southern Mexico, they carved huge stone heads to praise their rulers.

Both the Mayans and Aztecs
used cocoa beans to make a drink
known as chocolatl. The beans
were dried and crushed, and then
mixed with water. The Mayans
drank chocolatl hot, whilst the
Aztecs drank it cold.

Often flavourings, such as chilli or vanilla, were added. Nevertheless, the taste must have been very bitter.
In fact, the word chocolatl is said to mean "bitter water".

Chilli peppers

Vanilla pods

Chocolatl was served on special occasions, such as rituals and royal feasts. The mixture was usually poured from a height into the drinking vessel to make a thick foam on the top.

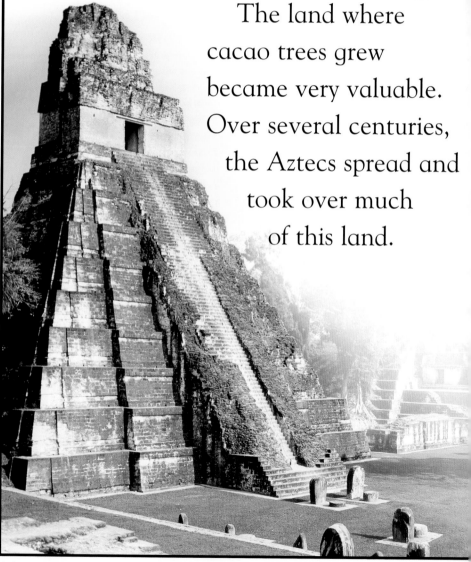

Both the Mayans and Aztecs used cocoa beans as money. They also gave beans as special gifts, and as offerings to the gods.

The land where cacao trees grew became very valuable. Over several centuries, the Aztecs spread and took over much of this land.

They collected taxes from the people in the form of cocoa beans. Their Aztec kings filled storehouses with the precious beans. People say that the emperor Montezuma had more than 960 million beans in his storehouses.

Emperor Montezuma

Army food supplies

Some of Montezuma's cocoa beans were made into wafers for his army. This was an early type of instant cocoa mix.

To Europe and beyond

In 1492, Christopher Columbus became the first European to sail to the Americas. During his fourth and final voyage to the New World in 1502, his ship came across a Mayan trading canoe full of cargo. Columbus ordered his crew to capture it.

Columbus's son, Ferdinand, wrote that among the loot taken from the canoe were "almonds". Ferdinand noticed that the Mayans treated them with great care. These "almonds" were, of course, cocoa beans. Although Columbus took some back to Spain, both he and the Spanish king were far too interested in gold and other treasures to take much notice of the small brown beans.

Other explorers soon followed Columbus to the New World. In 1519, the Spanish explorer Hernando Cortés arrived in Mexico. The Aztec emperor, Montezuma, served him a feast with chocolatl to drin

But Cortés had come to Mexico to claim the land for Spain, and by 1521 he had conquered the great Aztec nation. The Spanish explorers took on some Aztec customs, such as using cocoa beans as money. The taste of chocolatl was too bitter for them at first, but by adding sugar to sweeten it, the exotic drink became a favourite treat.

Sugar cane

Molinillo (mole-i-NEE-yo)

The Spanish explorers used a mixing stick called a molinillo to whip up the thick foam on top of their hot chocolatl.

The explorers brought cocoa beans back to Spain and introduced the hot, sweet drink to their country.

The chocolate drink soon became popular with rich families. Both cocoa beans and sugar had to be imported from the tropical rainforests in Central America, so chocolate was a luxury that only the rich could afford. People also thought that chocolate was good for their health.

Explorers from Spain were already busy in the New World, taking over land that was suitable for growing cacao trees. They could see that cocoa was going to be a money-making crop.

As there were few cocoa beans, the Spanish did not want to share the delights of drinking chocolate with other countries. It took nearly 100 years for the secret to spread to other parts of Europe. There is a legend that English pirates captured a Spanish ship carrying cocoa beans. The pirates thought that the beans were sheep droppings and they burned them!

However, by the 1650s, Europeans were drinking chocolate at fashionable cafés called chocolate houses. In 1660, Princess Maria Teresa of Spain married King Louis XIV of France. Maria Teresa liked chocolate so much that she had a special maid to make it for her. Soon, the rich French families began copying their new queen and liked the taste, too.

Chocolate pot

Tea from Asia and coffee from Africa were also popular in Europe at this time. Special jugs, such as this chocolate pot, were used to serve each drink.

Cocoa powder

By the 1700s, European settlers took the chocolate drink back across the Atlantic Ocean, where it became a popular treat in North America.

In 1765, the first American chocolate factory opened in Massachussetts, USA.

WALTER BAKER & CO'S MILLS - DORCHESTER, MASS.

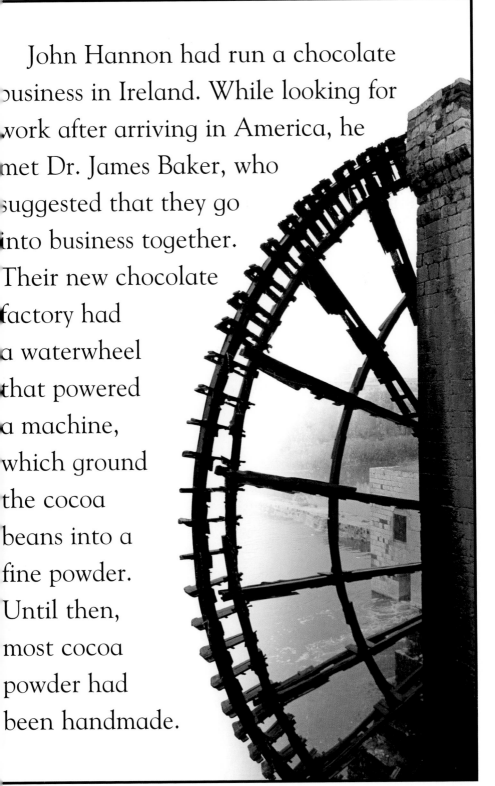

John Hannon had run a chocolate business in Ireland. While looking for work after arriving in America, he met Dr. James Baker, who suggested that they go into business together. Their new chocolate factory had a waterwheel that powered a machine, which ground the cocoa beans into a fine powder. Until then, most cocoa powder had been handmade.

Chocolate factories

In 1765, the Scottish inventor James Watt built a steam engine that made goods quickly and cheaply. Using a steam-powered chocolate grinder made chocolate a cheaper treat for everyone.

James Watt studying a steam engine

In 1828, the Dutch chemist Coenraad van Houten invented a chocolate press and this made

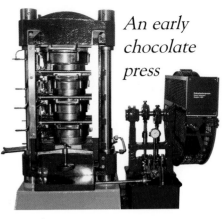

An early chocolate press

the chocolate taste better. Cocoa beans are made up of cocoa mass and fatty cocoa butter. Cocoa butter makes the chocolate greasy and doesn't mix well with water. The chocolate press separated out much of the cocoa butter. The result was chocolate that had a purer flavour and mixed easily with water.

The age of steam
Watt's steam engine led to the development of new machines, including the steam-powered fire pumper. It started the Industrial Revolution.

In the 1840s, Fry's chocolate company in England made the first solid chocolate for eating when they mixed cocoa powder and sugar with melted cocoa butter instead of water. The new mixture was poured into a mould and then cooled so the chocolate would harden.

The chocolate business boomed. Many different kinds of chocolate for eating were moulded into bars and other shapes – some were even filled with flavoured centres.

Chocolate was now cheaper for everyone, and sold to people of all ages. Cadbury's, another English company, made boxes of different chocolates. The boxes were decorated with pictures that children could cut out and keep. Chocolate was thought to be a healthy and delicious treat.

Chocolate was advertised as a healthy treat.

New towns

In England, Cadbury's and Rowntree's chocolate companies were run by families who took good care of their workers and built new towns for them.

Until 1875, all chocolate had been
what we now call plain or dark
chocolate. It was also coarse and gritty.
Then, two separate developments
happened in Switzerland.

Henri Nestlé was experimenting with
condensed milk for breakfast cereals
when his partner, Daniel Peter, suggested
adding condensed milk to chocolate. By
doing this, they invented milk chocolate.

Four years later, Rudolphe Lindt invented the "conche", a machine with rollers that moved backwards and forwards over the chocolate.

Cocoa mass

Model of Lindt's conche machine

The movement created friction and heat that broke down even the tiniest crumbs. The result was chocolate with a smooth, velvety texture.

In the United States, Milton Hershey opened his chocolate factory in 1905. Hershey built his factory in the dairy region of Pennsylvania, where he could easily get a large supply of milk. He mass produced milk chocolate by using the latest technology. One of his early successes was Hershey's Milk Chocolate with Almonds, which is still a bestseller in the US.

Hershey built a large, modern own for his vorkers with a hotel for visitors, a golf course and other leisure activities. Over the years, ourism has increased and the site has expanded into an amusement park. The town of Hershey has streets called Cocoa Avenue and Chocolate Avenue, and streetlamps shaped like Hershey's Kisses, one of the company's most popular products.

Making chocolate today

The average cacao tree only produces about 1 kilogram (2 lbs) of dried cocoa beans. More and more land is being taken over by cacao-tree growers to meet the huge demand for chocolate. Cacao trees now grow on plantations in many tropical rainforests within 20 degrees of the Equator. They need a hot, wet climate, low altitude and lots of midges to pollinate the blossoms.

North America

Central America

South America

Area where cacao trees are grown

Cacao trees are usually planted among taller trees, such as banana or coconut trees, which give them the shade they need. After about four years, pods begin growing on the young cacao trees.

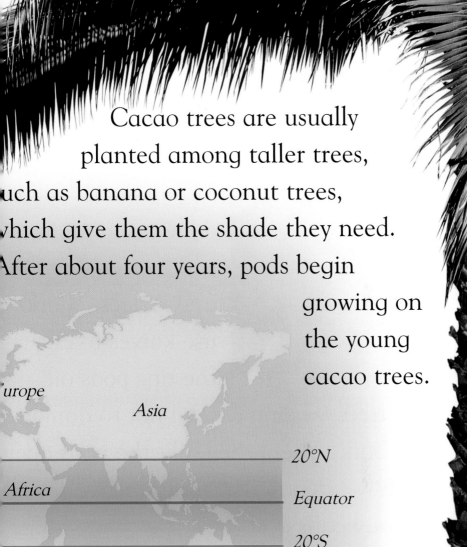

Europe

Asia

20°N

Africa

Equator

20°S

Australia

Organic chocolate

On some small farms, chemicals are not used and cacao trees are grown with native plants, which helps the environment. This chocolate is labelled "organic".

Despite the progress in making chocolate, cocoa farming must still be done by hand, as it was by the Mayans and Aztecs. Workers use knives to cut the ripe pods off the trees – being careful not to damage the bark. Then, they split the pods open with wooden mallets and remove the cocoa beans and the sticky white pulp.

Fairtrade

Chocolate that is labelled "Fairtrade" guarantees farmers a fair price for their cocoa beans. The label differs between countries, but the message is the same.

The beans and the pulp are heaped into big piles to ferment – a natural process that helps to bring out the flavour. After fermenting for about a week, the beans are dried in the sun and shipped to the chocolate factories.

At the factory, the beans are
cleaned and then roasted at a
very high temperature to bring
out their flavour.

A hulling machine then separates
the shell from the inside of the bean,
which is called the "nib".

The roast
machine

Cooking with cocoa

Cocoa powder is often used as an ingredient in other foods, such as biscuits, cakes and ice cream.

Only the nib of the bean is used to make chocolate. The nibs are ground in a machine until they turn into a thick paste. This paste is then pressed to separate the fatty cocoa butter from the cocoa mass.

To make cocoa powder, the cocoa mass is ground again into a fine powder. For chocolate-drink mixes, sugar is added to the cocoa powder.

The grinding machine

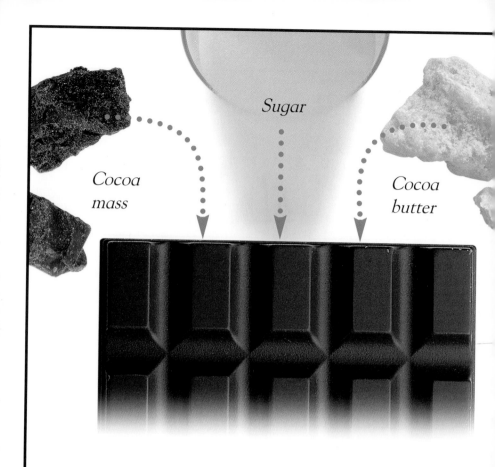

Cocoa mass

Sugar

Cocoa butter

Dark chocolate is cocoa mass mixed with sugar and some melted cocoa butter. The mixture is ground up and then put into a conche machine, where the rollers make the chocolate smooth. Then it is cooled in a process called "tempering" to give it the ideal texture.

To make milk chocolate, milk and sugar are mixed and heated, so that much of the liquid evaporates. This condensed milk is mixed with cocoa mass and dried into a crumbly mixture, which is then ground up and mixed with cocoa butter (often diluted with vegetable fat). Once flavourings, such as vanilla, have been added, the milk chocolate is conched and tempered.

Milk chocolate

Dark chocolate

White chocolate

White chocolate contains sugar, milk and cocoa butter, but no cocoa mass. Therefore, people say it is not "real" chocolate.

Assembly line of chocolate bars

Many chocolate bars are still made in moulds, but these days, the moulds are usually filled by machines. Some machines can fill more than 1,000 moulds in a minute – making the same number of bars! Nuts, caramel, and other ingredients can also be added during the moulding process. Then, the bars go through a cooling tunnel so the chocolate can harden.

Shaped chocolates

Chocolate shapes, such as eggs or rabbits, are also made using moulds. For hollow shapes, chocolate is squirted into a mould, which is then shaken to evenly coat the sides.

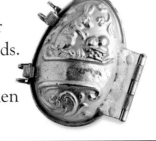

Chocolate is also used as a covering or biscuits, ice cream and cakes. The filling is dipped or squirted with chocolate until it is covered. This process is called "enrobing".

The next time you buy a chocolate bar, read the label before making your choice – the purer the chocolate, the better the bar.

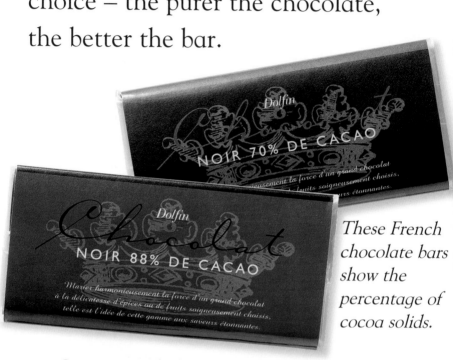

These French chocolate bars show the percentage of cocoa solids.

On most labels, cocoa mass and cocoa butter are measured together and called "cocoa solids". The percentage of cocoa solids in chocolate varies from about 15 to 75 per cent. Dark chocolate usually contains more cocoa solids than milk chocolate.

Modern chocolate has a bad press when it comes to healthy eating. However, many experts now agree that cocoa solids may be good for you, and that it is the sugar and other added ingredients that are fattening and unhealthy. It depends what kind of chocolate – and how much of it – you eat.

Soldiers' rations

During World War II, much of the chocolate produced in the USA was given to the soldiers for nourishment and strength as part of their daily rations.

CHOCOLATE IS A *Fighting* FOOD !

All kinds of chocolate

Today, there are many different kinds of chocolate treats — bars, biscuits, cakes, ice cream and many others.

In Mexico, where the cacao tree was first discovered, a popular dish is a chocolate-chilli sauce called molé poblano (mole-ay puh-BLAH-noh). It is made with plain chocolate and often eaten with chicken or turkey.

Molé poblano has a rich and spicy taste.

Chefs pouring chocolate into a 2.1-metres (7-ft) tall and 12.7-centimetres (5-in) deep heart-shaped mould.

Some chocolate creations are truly enormous! One record-breaking treat weighed 7,000 kilograms (15,400 lbs) – as much as 140,000 chocolate bars. But, like all chocolate, it began with a pod full of beans.

A sweet read

Roald Dahl was inspired by his childhood experiences as a taste tester in a sweet factory when writing his book *Charlie and the Chocolate Factory*.

Glossary

Cacao tree
The tree on which cocoa pods grow.

Chocolate press
A machine that squeezes the cocoa butter out of the chocolate, leaving the cocoa mass.

Chocolatl
The name used by the Mayans and Aztecs for their chocolate drink.

Cocoa beans
The seeds inside the cocoa pods that are used to make chocolate.

Cocoa butter
The fatty substance that is found in cocoa beans.

Cocoa mass
The part of chocolate that is left after the cocoa butter has been separated out.

Cocoa pods
The fruit of the cacao tree.

Cocoa solids
Cocoa mass and cocoa butter measured together.

Conche
A machine with rollers that heat and crush the crumbly chocolate mixture to make it smooth.

Condensed milk
Milk that has been heated so that much of the liquid evaporates.

Dark chocolate
Also known as plain chocolate, it is made from cocoa mass, cocoa butter and sugar.

Enrobing
Covering a food such as ice cream, cakes or biscuits with chocolate.

Fermentation
A natural process by which the cocoa beans break down, making the chocolate flavour stronger.

Hulling
To separate the nib from the bean shell.

Mesoamerica
Historic area of what is now Mexico and Central America, where the Olmecs, Mayans and Aztecs lived.

Midges
Small flying insects that carry pollen between the blossoms on the cacao tree. They pollinate the flowers, allowing the pods to grow.

Milk chocolate
Chocolate to which milk has been added during manufacturing.

Nib
The inside of the cocoa bean, after the shell has been removed.

Pulp
The soft part of a fruit. In a cocoa pod, sticky white pulp covers the cocoa beans.

Rainforest
A thick forest area where the climate is hot and damp.

Tempering
Manufacturing process in which chocolate is carefully cooled to give it the right texture.